FABULOUS BEASTS
MYTHS AND LEGENDS

Translated by Abigail Frost

Text by Claude-Catherine Ragache

Illustrations by Marcel Laverdet

Series edited by Gilles Ragache

CHERRYTREE BOOKS

A Cherrytree Book

Adapted by A S Publishing
from *Les Animaux Fantastiques*
published by Hachette
© 1991, Hachette, Paris

First published 1994
by Cherrytree Press Ltd
a subsidiary of
The Chivers Company Ltd
Windsor Bridge Road
Bath, Avon BA2 3AX

Copyright © Cherrytree Press Ltd 1994

British Library Cataloguing in Publication Data
Ragache, Claude-Catherine
  Fabulous Beasts.—(Myths & Legends Series)
  I. Title   II. Frost, Abigail   III. Laverdet, Marcel Series
  398.24

  ISBN 0-7451-5232-5

Printed in Hong Kong by Colorcraft Ltd

▷ CONTENTS ◁

THE RAINBOW SERPENT

When the world was first made, all the birds of the Amazon forests had the same dull plumage. The forest Indians never hunted them. But, at the bottom of the great river, lived a huge, ferocious serpent.

If any living creature dared go near the river, the serpent would rise up and swallow them. But humans had to collect water to drink and catch fish for food. So they called on the birds to help them fight the serpent.

Deep down in the water, the serpent saw them gather on the bank above. It thought greedily of the splendid meal they would make. But, poking its head above the surface, it saw that the Indians had bows and arrows and the birds had sharp beaks. It decided to stay under the water.

On the bank, the comrades decided someone would have to dive in the river. 'Our skill is fighting on land,' said the men. 'You shall have the honour of diving.'

'No, no,' said the birds. 'Pray excuse us. We only know how to fight in the air.' They argued long and politely, until at last a cormorant spoke: 'Shut up! Someone's got to do it, so I will! Get ready to help me bring the serpent up to the surface.'

Quickly the cormorant dived in, and marvelled at the sight below: the serpent's scaly skin was in all the colours of the rainbow. Nobody had ever seen more than its grim black head before. But the bird remembered his task and drove his sharp beak into the serpent's head, killing it at once.

The Indians threw their fishing nets into the water and drew the serpent up. Everyone gasped when they saw its body. Some of the men began to skin it – but the cormorant

Only the cormorant was brave enough to tackle the serpent.

demanded its skin as the victor's right. 'Come and get it, then!' cried the men, thinking such a little bird could never carry the huge skin away. But all the birds helped, and gripping it with their claws, flew away with it. The men fired arrows after them – but they got away.

Deep in the forest the birds shared out the serpent's rainbow colours. Now some had red feathers, some blue, some purple. But the brave cormorant, who had won the prize, was left till last, when all that was left was the black of the serpent's head. But, being a wise bird, he was pleased. Since then, the other birds have been hunted for their feathers, but not him.

THE FROG WHO LAUGHED

One day, a little frog simply went crazy. It was just an ordinary frog, small and quiet. That was the trouble: nobody took any notice of it. It had to take a lot of care not to get trodden on by the other animals. A wild idea came into its head. It thought of a way of making everyone pay attention to it. It would become big and powerful. Yes, the others would have to learn to treat it with respect!

First the frog went to a pond, and drank up all the water in it. Then it drank up another pond, and another. Then it drank up all the water in all the lakes, then all the rivers, then all the seas. And with each lot of water it swallowed, it swelled up and grew bigger and bigger.

Slowly the earth began to dry up, as the frog drank all the water. The plants began to wilt, and the other animals could find nothing to eat or drink. But the frog went on drinking and swelling up regardless. Soon it was taller than the tallest trees and wider than the biggest mountains. Its bright green skin was stretched like a balloon and it was so heavy it could not move. It just sat there, watching the world with staring eyes and a crazy sense of pride.

The huge frog could see all the other animals standing in a circle way down below. They were so small and so far away from its head that it could not hear them talking. 'We must do something, we're dying of thirst!' said one. 'But what can we do? It's huge!' said another. Then they began to think. The frog was swollen up to bursting with all that water. Perhaps they could make it burst with laughter. One little creature, with its last strength, started to dance, pull funny faces, and clown around. Soon all the animals were laughing – except the huge, impassive frog. Others tried silly contortions; everyone laughed even more, except the frog.

At last a snake, usually the most cold and solemn of all the animals, tried to make the frog laugh. It stood on its tail and wriggled in a ridiculous manner.

Success! The frog began to laugh; and once it had started it could not stop. Tears sprouted from its eyes and water flooded from its huge mouth. As it laughed it shrank, and shrank, and shrank. Soon the seas, rivers and lakes were full again, and once again all was well with the world.

The fat frog laughed until it cried.

▷ THE WHOWIE ◁

Once upon a time, long before humans appeared on earth, all the animals talked in the same language. The tortoises said hello to the birds, the koalas helped the kangaroos to look after their babies, the duck-billed platypuses raced the fish in the rivers. They all worked together and shared everything, living in harmony along the riverbank.

It was paradise by day, but when the sun went down in the evening, panic set in. Mother animals hastened to gather up their babies, while all the others gathered wood, leaves, and anything else they could find to hide themselves. Dark, silent night fell over the riverbank, and the animals kept still in their nests, hardly daring to move – for fear of the dreadful Whowie monster.

Out of a dark cave in the rocks came a huge and frightening shape, like a gigantic dragon. The enormous creature moved silently and swiftly down to the riverbank. Once here, it bent down its head, turned over a nest and ate whatever it found. It growled, as it satisfied its appetite, and then left the bank in silence.

The Whowie was about twenty feet long, and had six legs. It had a huge head with strong jaws to crunch its food, and cruel claws on its feet. By day, it slept in its sinister cave, but at night, when other animals slept, it went out to seek its prey.

One night, the animals had had enough. Too many baby animals had been eaten. But how could they defeat such a huge, cruel enemy?

'It is big,' said one. 'But we are many, many more. If we all unite, we can attack it while it is asleep. I have a plan.'

So the kangaroo spoke to the platypus, and the platypus spoke to the fish, and the fish told the birds, and the birds told the wombats, and the wombats told the koalas, and so on, until all the animals knew what to do. And they gathered on the riverbank, ready to act.

At mid-day, when the sun was high and bright in the sky and the Whowie was sleeping deeply, they all brought branches to its cave, and piled them high. Soon there was an enormous bonfire outside the cave. One of the birds knew the secret of fire, and quickly lit the

pile. Thick smoke soon filled the cave, and the Whowie woke up, choking. Its coughs shook the rocks and the earth below them. But it did not suffocate. The fire burned for seven days and seven nights. The Whowie got hotter and hotter in its cave. Its scales turned red with the heat. At last, it could bear it no longer. It ran out of its cave, ignoring the terrified animals, and threw itself in the river, where it drowned.

All the animals celebrated that night, and lived in peace for many more years.

The Whowie's coughing shook the land.

▷ THE STORM-CAMEL ◁

Long ago, among the nomad tribes of Central Asia, lived a hero called Merkut. Though young, he had done many great deeds, and feared neither man nor beast. Some said he had even fought giants and won.

But there was one thing that troubled Merkut: storms. He did not want to be struck by lightning. He knew it could strike anywhere without warning, and he was as vulnerable as the feeblest child in the tribe. He could not bear this thought, and longed to find a way to protect himself.

Like everyone in his tribe, he knew who was to blame for the thunderstorms that rent the skies on hot summer nights: a camel! But it was no ordinary camel: it was an incarnation of the devil. Whenever this spirit of evil entered a river or a lake to cool down, it caused a storm. Steam came out of its nostrils and made a thick cloud which carried it up to the sky. But the camel could not keep its balance on the cloud's soft, round surface, and rolled to the right and left. Sooner or later, it would fall back down to earth, grinding its teeth thunderously and spitting out flashing fire. Sometimes the camel broke a tooth; if you found one, it brought good luck, so long as you did not tell anyone you had found it.

One summer day a heavy storm broke. While the rest of the tribe huddled in their tents, Merkut mounted his horse and rode off towards the thunder. Under the eye of the storm, he tethered his horse among the rocks, and waited. There above him was the camel, wobbling on its cloud and looking as if it was about to fall any minute.

Soon, spitting blinding lightning, the devilish camel landed by Merkut. Quickly he leapt on its back. The enraged animal bucked and wheeled in the hope of dismounting him, but Merkut sat firm between its humps. Its nostrils began to steam, and soon the pair were rising up on a storm cloud.

The camel bucked and writhed for five days and five nights, but it could not throw Merkut. On the earth below, people wondered why the storm was going on so long. Was it the end of the world? Merkut's back and arms were aching agonisingly. How long would he have to ride this terrible creature?

But his mount was as tired as he. At last it spoke, and begged for mercy. 'I will leave you in peace,' said Merkut, 'as long as you promise never to throw your thunder and lightning at me!' 'Agreed,' said the camel. 'But how shall I know it's you?' 'Easy. I'll simply call out "I'm Merkut, I'm Merkut!" and you will take your cloud away.' So the bargain was made. The camel took Merkut back to earth, and Merkut no longer had to fear storms. And for ever after, the people of his tribe used to shout 'I'm Merkut!' when they saw a thunder-cloud, and bang their cooking-pots until the cloud rolled away.

The furious camel tried hard to shake Merkut from its back.

11

▷ THE BLUE LIONS ◁

At the bottom of a great African river lived a pride of lions. They were much like ordinary lions, except that their fur was deep blue. The lions were always hungry, so every night they swam out and hunted for prey. At the back of their den, which was hidden behind a curtain of waterweeds, was a row of huge jars. These were their larder.

One night one of them caught a new-born human baby. It was still alive, for this was a magic river, and nothing ever drowned in it. The lion did not kill the baby but took it back to the den and put it in a jar. It would keep better that way.

The baby was the son of a poor woman whose husband had run away. Broken-hearted, she threw first her baby, then herself, into the river. Nothing the villagers could do could stop her. They ran off and found her husband and told him what had happened because of his faithlessness. He was overcome with guilt, and set off at once to find his wife and baby. He took with him, for safety, a magic horn, from a kind of antelope his people called a ngona.

Night fell and the water grew dark, but the horn glowed mysteriously to light the way. The man spotted his wife's footprints along the riverbed. Soon he caught up with her, and took her hand tenderly. They went on together to the blue lions' den. They trod carefully, fearing to disturb any lions that were hiding in the waterweeds. They knew they had only a short time to find their baby before the creatures came back from hunting. When they reached the den, they looked carefully to make sure all the lions were out. Then they dashed inside.

Their hearts sank. There were dozens of jars to search, and so little time! The mother began to cry at the difficulty of their task. 'Don't worry,' said her husband, showing her the magic ngona-horn and pointing it towards the lions' larder. 'Magic horn! Tell me where my son is hidden!' And out from one of the jars came a strange little voice: 'In here! In here!' Inside was their baby, safe and sound.

'Quick, let's get out of here!' said the father. But he was too late. A huge old blue lion was blocking the entrance. The couple had been too busy to hear him approach.

'Get in that jar!' roared the old lion. 'Now!' And he forced them back into the cave and into the biggest jar.

But once again the magic ngona-horn came to the rescue. The man carefully pointed it and drew it downwards, first over the baby, then over his wife, and lastly over himself. Each shrank to a tiny size. Now they could all creep inside the hollow of the horn.

At dawn all the other blue lions came home, eager for their breakfast. The old lion proudly offered them his catch. Slavering, they opened the jar – to find nothing but a dry old horn! One lion angrily bit it; but instead of crunching it up, he broke his teeth on it. Disgusted, he spat it out – and so the horn flew out of the den, up to the surface and landed on the riverbank! Safe on land, the family quickly regained their proper size. Their adventure was the talk of the village. It was a rare thing to have seen the blue lions – and even rarer to live to tell the tale.

Too late! The blue lion blocked the way from its lair.

The firebird lifted the gentle dragon high into the sky.

THE TERRIBLE TENGU

The little raindragon slept peacefully on a mossy bank beneath a rosebush. The dragon loved his home, in a quiet monastery garden. The monks were all his friends, and they looked after him well. His best friend was the monk who looked after the garden. He always said hello as he tended the plants.

Though he was only young, the dragon had (like all dragons of his kind) the power to draw rain from the clouds and keep the drought away.

Suddenly a frightening roar woke the dragon. The garden was dark, and hot as a furnace. The terrified dragon tried to hide under a rock, but too late. He felt his body gripped by fearsome claws as he was lifted high into the air. He had been caught by the terrible Tengu, the cruel firebird, bringer of drought and deadly foe of the raindragons!

The monster flapped its wings and flew quickly away from the monastery, over great forests and high mountains to a vast, burning desert. Here it let the poor dragon fall like a stone into the depths of a ravine. Bruised and shaken, he lay there waiting to die. How could a creature of water survive in this dry, hot land?

Leaving the dragon to his fate, the Tengu flew back to the monastery. The gardener stood sadly by his vegetable plots, wondering where his friend had gone. When he saw the firebird, he knew what had happened. He raged at the Tengu, shaking his fist and brandishing his watering-pot angrily.

The Tengu was annoyed. How dare this tiny little man shout at him! The bird dived down and seized the monk in its claws, then flew him to the desert and dropped him down, near where the dragon lay dying.

The monk spread out his arms, and the long, wide sleeves of his robe caught the air and carried him down gently to the ravine's edge. He still had his watering-pot in his hand, with a little water left in it. Praying that it was not too late, he poured the water down on to the dragon's head.

The very first drop began to revive the dragon. He drew a deep breath and stood up. Then, with a flick of his tail, he jumped up out of the ravine, and told his friend the gardener to get on his back. Then he rose up into the sky and flew quickly home. The terrible Tengu was never seen again in the area. It knew when it was beaten.

A drop of water from the gardener's pot revived the dying dragon.

▷ BOONGURUNGURU ◁

Proudly, young Basania set out into the deep forest around the village. His father had sent him out for the first time to cut palms to mend the roof of their hut. At last he was big enough to use a machete!

Soon, Basania found a clump of palm trees and climbed right up the biggest. He could see the village, and all his friends and family, looking tiny. He cut down a few branches and watched them fall, then climbed down and tried the next tree.

Soon, he felt tired. The heavy machete made his arms ache. It was time to go home. He climbed one last tree, and looked around. Where had the village gone? He looked on every side, but could not see so much as a plume of smoke.

Basania looked up. The sky was dark and the treetops shook in the wind. There was a storm coming up. Sliding down the long trunk, he heard a terrible growling sound. He knew what it was: the voice of the Boongurunguru, a fierce and gigantic wild beast that everyone dreaded meeting. As it ran through the forest with its ferocious young, the earth shook under their feet.

Trembling with fear, Basania hid in the undergrowth. The noises came nearer, and soon he could see the beasts' eyes amongst the dark leaves. He squeezed up small, hoping they would not notice him. Then he saw where they were heading: towards his village. The old people said the Boongurunguru could destroy everything. Bravely, the boy decided to show himself and draw them away from his home.

Basania began to sing at the top of his voice. He could hear trees crashing down in the dark forest, and see the animals' eyes grow brighter.

Plucking up all his courage, he faced the terrible enemy – and saw that they were no more than a family of wild pigs. The piglets were no bigger than rats.

Now he remembered that the old stories said that if anyone had the courage to face the Boongurunguru, it would shrink away before his sight. Well, the legend must be true. Just to be sure, Basania threw his machete at the Boongurunguru. It ran off into the forest, defeated.

Back at home, Basania's father was angry. Where were the palm branches? What had happened to the precious machete? Basania kept quiet. If he said what he had seen, flying serpents would devour his home. He knew it was true – the old stories said so.

The Boongurunguru tramped through the undergrowth.

▷ THE ROKH ◁

Budak Yoid longed to learn the secrets of metalwork, but his six elder brothers drove him away from their forge, saying he was too young. So at night, he would sneak in and secretly work on leftover pieces of iron. He had watched his brothers at work all his life and quickly learned all their skills.

After many nights' work, he proudly finished the piece he had dreamed of, and called his brothers to see. They could scarcely believe their eyes when Budak showed them a beautiful cutlass, the biggest ever made in the forge! Its blade shone in the firelight like a mirror. When Budak told them he had made the cutlass himself they laughed; but they had to believe him when they found that only he could lift it.

Now Budak wanted to go out into the world to seek his fortune. As he made his farewells, he pointed out a flowering bush he had planted in the garden, and said, 'While the flowers are blooming, you will know I am all right. But if they start to fall, that means I am in danger.' The boy set off through the jungle, cutting his way with his cutlass.

The cutlass was a wonderful weapon indeed; it had secret powers. It could change its size to order. One day, when Budak had to cross a river, the cutlass grew long enough to make a bridge, then, when he was safe on the other side, changed back again. When not in use, it would fly up into the sky, but as soon as Budak called for it, it was in his hand.

One day Budak passed through a silent, deserted city. In the centre was a magnificent palace, which was deserted too. He searched through all its courts and rooms, but found no living creature there.

In one courtyard, he found a huge drum. Just to break the silence, he began to beat it and sing a song. Then he heard a little voice, which seemed to come from the drum. He looked inside, and to his astonishment he found a lovely young princess.

'Save me!' she cried. 'I am the last person alive here! A monstrous bird called the Rokh has eaten everyone else.' She explained that the Rokh came every night; many heroes had tried to kill it, but none had succeeded. It had seven ravenous heads.

As she spoke, a dark shadow fell over the palace and a heavy wind rushed through its courtyards. The Rokh was coming. The princess quickly hid in the drum, while Budak summoned his cutlass to his hand. The Rokh was coming closer. It had not expected a fight. One head darted near; but soon it was lying lifeless on the ground. Budak fought all night until he had cut off all the monster's heads. But falling dead from the sky, the bird trapped Budak under one of its enormous wings.

The princess ran to his aid, but could not lift the wing. At home, Budak's brothers saw the flowers fading on the magic bush. They rode out, following his tracks, and at last came to the palace, and were able to lift off the carcass.

Safe at last, Budak and the princess were married. Their children, and their children's children, brought life again to the deserted city.

Alone, with only his magic cutlass, Budak faces the deadly Rokh.

18

THE FLYING MONKEY

Prince Rama was distraught with grief. The demon Ravana – who had ten heads and many, many arms – had tricked him into leaving Princess Sita, his wife, alone in the forest. Then Ravana had taken the shape of a bird, swooped down and carried her up into the sky. Rama went into the mountains and asked the king of the monkeys if he knew where Sita might be.

'Perhaps,' said the king. 'A few days ago, Ravana's chariot flew over this peak. A woman leaned out and threw down these.' Rama recognised his wife's jewels and veil. The king offered to lend him his best general, Hanumat, and an army to help rescue Sita.

Hanumat was the son of the wind god. He could fly, and cross great distances in a single stride. Rama, Hanumat and the monkey army searched all over India, but they could not find Sita. At last they reached the sea. A huge, ancient vulture whispered to Hanumat. With his sharp eyes, he had seen Ravana take Sita to his castle on the island of Lanka.

Hanumat gave a mighty leap and landed on the island. All the roads were defended by demons and armoured elephants. But he had another trick to play; he made himself very small and slipped into Ravana's castle unseen. Here he found Sita, and changed back to his right size. But she refused to climb on his back to escape, so he went back to get Rama and his army.

The sea was full of monsters, but the monkeys set to work building a causeway of stones across it. Then they all surged over to Lanka. The demons met them head-on. Hanumat battled his way through, hurling rocks down from a great height, killing the demons and clearing a path for Rama to fight Ravana hand to hand. He easily killed the demon with his magic sword.

But the victory was hard won. All Hanumat's soldier-monkeys were dead or badly wounded. So the general made another great leap, up to the Himalayas, thousands of miles away and the highest mountains in the world. Here there grew magic healing plants. When the plants saw him, they hid. Wasting no time, Hanumat tore off the mountain-top and carried it to Lanka, and used the plants to heal the monkeys' wounds and bring the dead back to life.

Fearlessly, the monkeys face a sea full of monsters.

PEGASUS AND THE CHIMERA

When the Greek hero Perseus killed the Gorgon Medusa – who had snakes growing from her head like hair, and whose eyes turned anyone who looked at her to stone – he cut off her hideous head for a trophy. Two figures leapt up from her neck: Chrysador, a warrior, armed with a golden sword, and Pegasus, a magnificent horse with wings.

Soon people came from far and wide to try to capture the wondrous Pegasus. He was a shy, wild creature, and they had to wait a long time for a glimpse of him. And when a hunter moved towards him, the graceful white horse just spread his wings and flew away.

Among the hunters was a young man called Bellerophon. Handsome and clever, he had many jealous enemies. One day he was falsely accused of a crime, and sent into exile until he had performed many brave deeds. One was to kill the Chimera, a fire-breathing monster with three heads – a lion's, a goat's and a dragon's.

It was impossible to fight the Chimera on the ground – but from the air? This thought led Bellerophon to Pegasus. For days he followed the winged horse's tracks, but had no luck. Pegasus seemed to be teasing him, letting him get almost close enough to stroke him, then suddenly flying away.

Bellerophon went to ask the goddess Athena for help. But, tired from his quest, he fell asleep in her temple. He woke hours later, thinking he heard a voice. But nobody was there. On the ground lay a gift from Athena – a golden halter.

Next day, Pegasus was drinking at a stream. Bellerophon tiptoed up and slipped the halter over the horse's head. Pegasus did not resist, tamed by Athena's power.

Now, for the first time, Bellerophon mounted Pegasus and ordered him to fly. He sat between Pegasus's beautiful wings, marvelling at the view beneath. Down below the countryside changed from lush green to burnt brown as they neared the Chimera's lair. The air smelt of sulphurous smoke and the clouds were black.

Pegasus circled slowly above the monster as his rider aimed his bow. The Chimera roared,

and blew out flames – but they did not reach high enough. Bellerophon let fly a quiverful of arrows tipped with lead. The metal melted in the heat of the monster's breath – and killed it agonisingly.

Bellerophon's enemies saw that he was protected by the gods, and stopped troubling him. But he had one enemy left: his own pride. He began to think he was the equal of the gods, and tried to fly on Pegasus up to their home on Mount Olympus. Zeus, king of the gods, killed him with a thunderbolt for his arrogance. But Pegasus lived for ever after on Mount Olympus. He became a messenger for the gods, and the protector of poets.

Seated safely on the back of Pegasus, Bellerophon fires arrow after arrow until the Chimera is dead.

GIANTS OF THE SEA

Long ago people believed that the earth was flat. Sailors feared that if they sailed too far their ships might fall over the edge of the world, where who knew what horrible monsters might devour them. But all the sailors were sure that, even without going over the edge, the sea held quite enough monsters for anyone.

Nowadays, with modern diving equipment to help, scientists can study the amazing real creatures that live in the depths of the sea. Some are stranger than anything the sailors imagined. But they hold no terrors for us; they are adapted for life in deep water, and rarely, if ever, come anywhere near the surface.

Here are some creatures from old books of natural history and sailors' legends.

The Kraken and the giant squid

Octopuses and squids have given rise to many legends. Some North American Indians who lived by the Pacific Ocean believed in gigantic squid-like animals, which brought good luck. The chiefs of these tribes used to bathe near the creatures' haunts, to show their followers their power.

Ancient Norwegian sailors feared the Kraken, a monstrous animal like an octopus, which drew fish towards it with its enormous tentacles. The crews of fishing vessels knew that where the Kraken was they would get a rich catch; but they kept a careful watch for any movement in the water that might mean the Kraken was rising.

The Ziph and the sea-serpent

The Ziph was a strange fish with webbed feet and a razor-sharp pointed beak. It was thought to live in the cold seas of the northern hemisphere. In the picture it is fighting a sea-serpent.

Nearly all sea-faring peoples have stories about sea-serpents. The Vikings believed that one of them, the Midgard Serpent, circled the earth at the bottom of a great sea. Some ancient Muslim sailors believed in a seven-headed sea-serpent called the Tennin. Usually it lived deep down in the water, but sometimes it came ashore, where it knocked down trees, whole towns and even mountains with its long black tail. The monster Leviathan, described in the Bible, was said to swallow water and then spew it up again. It was often blamed for whirlpools and tidal waves.

The Trolual

Troluals, or devil-whales, were thought to live in the seas around Iceland. They were as big as mountains, and liked to play with ships, picking them up, capsizing them or throwing them into the air like balls. Sailors would try to frighten them away by blowing trumpets, or distract them by throwing barrels overboard, while the ship made its escape.

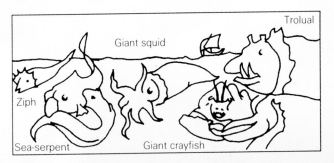

ARION AND THE DOLPHIN

A little ship sailed from Sicily to the Greek islands, carrying an important passenger: the poet and musician Arion, returning to his home. He had brought aboard so much luggage that the crew were sure he must be very rich. The poet sat happily at the prow playing his lyre. He was composing songs inspired by the beauty of the sea. Dolphins played in the water below, attracted by the music.

Suddenly, Arion felt a blow to his head. The next thing he knew he was being thrown overboard, half-stunned and unable to resist.

The ship quickly sped away. The wicked sailors were soon breaking open the chests he had brought with him, hoping to find plenty of money in them.

Arion did not have the strength to swim. He held on to his lyre, and strummed the strings as he sank below the water. Suddenly he found himself carried gently back to the surface. One of the dolphins which had enjoyed his music was rescuing him. The dolphin carried him on its back to the shore, where the thieves were soon caught.

Arion is rescued by the dolphins that swam to hear his music.

ANDROMEDA AND THE SEA MONSTER

Perseus, the Greek hero who killed the Gorgon (see page 22), was returning home along the African coast. He wore the presents the gods had given him when he went to fight the Gorgon: a helmet which made him invisible, and winged sandals which allowed him to fly. Down below he heard cries of fear. He looked down, and saw a beautiful princess chained to a rock.

Perseus removed his helmet, so that the princess could see him, and asked her what was happening. 'My name is Andromeda,' she said. 'My father is the king of this land. I am chained here to be eaten by a sea-monster. Whoever you are, you cannot save me. The gods have ordered my fate, because my mother said she was more beautiful than Hera, queen of the gods. If you should break my chains, Hera will punish you. But if you can kill the monster, my father will reward you. But you must be quick! Here comes the monster.'

With his helmet on his head, Perseus gradually became invisible.

Perseus hastened to the palace, and offered to kill the monster – provided that he could marry Andromeda. The king agreed. When Perseus returned to the shore, he saw a raging storm. The monster was slowly moving close to the terrified Andromeda. Quickly the hero put on his magic helmet and sandals, drew his sword and flew out to sea.

A great tidal wave broke on the shore, and the monster rose from the foaming water, its mouth open ready to eat the princess. It arched its back ready to strike – and then stopped and fell back as it felt a blow from the sword of its unseen foe. Enraged with pain, it rose again, and once again fell back. At last, it was mortally wounded, and sank far beneath the waves.

Perseus removed his helmet as it sank, so that the monster could see who had killed it. Then he unchained Andromeda and took her home to claim her hand in marriage.

ALEXANDER AND THE SEA MONSTERS

Alexander the Great, ruler of Macedonia, died in 323 BC. He had built up a great empire by conquest, travelling as far as India in his campaigns, and died wishing there were more worlds for him to conquer. Long after his death, he was still famous and revered, and new legends about him kept being invented.

One of the stories told about Alexander was about the building of his capital city, Alexandria. The city was on the coast of Egypt, and had among other things the greatest library in the world. While the builders were working on its harbour, they were beset by a problem. Every night, sea-monsters came and destroyed all the work the builders had done by day.

Alexander decided to take on the monsters himself. He asked one of his cleverest engineers to build him a barrel of pure crystal, lit from the inside with lanterns. It was linked to a ship on the surface by an enormous gold chain.

Alexander and two artists got into the barrel and were let down to the bottom of the sea. As the barrel slowly travelled down, the three saw all sorts of strange fish. The deeper they went, the stranger the sea-creatures became, until at last they reached the bottom and found the monsters.

There they were, chewing away on the wooden piles that held up the harbour buildings. Some had noses like saws, others razor-sharp teeth, and others heads like hammers. They were using these 'tools' to destroy the harbour. One of the monsters was so long it took three days and three nights to swim past them.

Safe in the barrel, Alexander and his companions made careful drawings of the creatures. Then they signalled to the surface for the chain to be winched up.

Back on land, Alexander gave the drawings to the finest sculptors of his empire. They used all their skill to make exact likenesses of all the monsters. Nothing so hideous had ever been seen!

When the sculptures were finished, Alexander had them all set up beside the sea. Then he ordered the builders to start work on the harbour again. That night, the monsters came up as before to destroy the harbour buildings. But a terrifying sight met their eyes! They swam away, determined never again to go near the place which had such hideous guards. They did not realise that they had been frightened away by their own ugly faces!

Safe in his crystal barrel, Alexander marvels at the grotesque underwater carpenters.

THE MAMITS AND THE MAGIC CAULDRON

Er-Toshtuk was a giant of superhuman strength. He had a magic horse, called Tchal-Konyrouk, who never grew tired. He could speak to humans, and lived on magic herbs, which he always chewed seven times.

One day, as the horse and rider galloped over a grassy plain, the earth opened up and they fell into a mysterious underground country. It was ruled by a cruel blue giant. The peaceful people who lived there, the Mamits, cowered before him. As Er-Toshtuk and Tchal-Konyrouk landed, four Mamits came to their side. 'Welcome to the Underworld!' said one. 'Your fame has spread here. I am Mamit-Knowall. My friends are Mamit-Fleetfoot, Mamit-Sharpears, and Mamit-Sharpeyes.'

The Mamits guided Er-Toshtuk and Tchal-Konyrouk deep into the Underworld. One day they met a beautiful young girl, who fell in love with Er-Toshtuk, and spoke of him to her father – the blue giant. Fearing that this hero might replace him, the giant had his daughter bound in heavy chain-mail, so she could not lead Er-Toshtuk to his camp.

But Er-Toshtuk knew what he had done, thanks to Mamit-Sharpears' and Mamit-Sharpeyes' wondrous senses. They all set off for the camp at once.

The giant was waiting with an evil grin. He told Er-Toshtuk he could marry his daughter on one condition. He must bring back a magic cauldron which warriors from the world above had seized. The cauldron cooked wonderful food out of nothing; but it was hard to get hold of because it had forty handles – and each was a living demon. The cauldron was now at the bottom of a great lake in the desert. Er-Toshtuk agreed to the quest. 'Goodbye,' said the giant. 'And *bad luck!*'

After forty days' ride, the party reached the lake shore, where they saw a black stone, inscribed 'Point of No Return'. Here the last of the warriors who had stolen the magic cauldron had perished. Tchal-Konyrouk spoke to his master: 'Let me go into the lake and find the cauldron, while you keep watch. If you see black foam on the water, it means I am dead; if red, I am wounded; and if white, I have won the cauldron.'

The horse swam down to where the cauldron lay. Its first handle, a demon which breathed poison, rose up to fight. Waiting anxiously on the shore, Mamit-Sharpears cried: 'Tchal-Konyrouk is in trouble. I can hear that he can't breathe properly.' And red foam appeared on the water. But then Mamit-Sharpeyes spoke: 'He's won! He's got the cauldron! See, the foam is now white!'

Tchal-Konyrouk surfaced, the cauldron between his teeth. Back in the Underworld, the blue giant grudgingly agreed to see them. But before the giant could take the cauldron, the horse threw it at him. It exploded, killing the giant, and freeing the Underworld from his tyranny at last.

The Mamits watch as the magic horse tells his master that he will dive down to get the cauldron.

The golden ram, bringer of storms.

▷ THE GOLDEN BOAR ◁

The Norse god of fire, Loki, was a cruel trickster. He made a bet with two dwarf smiths that they could not make two magical objects: a ring which brought its owner ever-growing riches, and a living golden boar.

The dwarfs, who were proud of their skill, took up the challenge. But Loki had no intention of letting them win. As they worked, first one, then the other, was stung by a huge horse-fly.

Every time they raised their hammers, the fly would bite again! They kept having to stop and scratch themselves. While one worked, the other would be chasing round their workshop trying to swat the fly. They began to suspect the truth: the fly was Loki, who had changed his shape to cheat them.

But in spite of it all, they finished the job. Now the golden boar pulls the god Frey's chariot across the sky. To mortals it looks like a shooting star.

AFRICA

▷ THE GOLDEN RAM ◁

What a terrible noise! Up in the sky, an old ewe was arguing, as she often did, with her son, a ram with a golden fleece. Down on earth the villagers gathered up their possessions, hoping the ewe would stop her rebellious son coming down.

His mother shouted and yelled at him not to go. Sometimes she got her way and sometimes she did not. When she did not, he would leap down in a blaze of lightning, bringing a terrible storm.

He was an angry beast! He would tear up trees as if they were blades of grass. Sometimes he would set a house on fire with his burning horns. Whatever happened, it was a disaster for humans when he arrived.

The dwarfs forged the
golden boar, despite
Loki's attempt to stop
them.

The Yeti, or 'abominable snowman'.

Unicorns

Chipique

Phoenix

Vouivre

LIVING LEGENDS?

The Chipique

This creature lives in the Zambezi at the foot of the great Victoria Falls in East Africa. Feared by all the local people, it is said to capsize boats and throw them back on land, while the crews drown in the rushing waters. Its scaly skin is easily mistaken for a rock as it lies in wait. Some European explorers of the nineteenth century scoffed at the local stories – until, they said, they saw the monster themselves!

The Vouivre

Fire-snake and water-snake in one, the Vouivre comes from southern France. Its winged body is surrounded by flames, and on its head is a shining precious stone. It loves to bathe in wells and fountains, and leaves the stone on land when it does. So anyone who knows where it bathes can take the valuable stone – provided the snake does not catch them!

The Yeti

This famous creature of the Himalaya mountains first came to the knowledge of Europeans in 1921, when a party led by the British climbers Mallory and Irvine attempted to reach the top of Mount Everest. On their journey, they noticed a gigantic footprint similar to a human one. They were surprised by the respect the Nepalese sherpas in their party paid to the print. When the news reached London, the creature gained the nickname 'abominable snowman'. Sadly, Mallory and Irvine died on the last stage of their journey.

According to the Nepalese people in the area, there are three kinds of Yeti. One is too small to bother humans, and another is up to three metres tall, but is vegetarian. The one to beware of is the middle-sized one, which eats people!

The Phoenix

The Greek historian Herodotus first described this fabulous bird, which was said to live in Egypt. It supposedly appears only once every five centuries to the people of Heliopolis, the Egyptian 'city of the Sun'. When it dies, it throws itself on the sun-god's altar, where its body burns away in the sacred flames. But out of the ashes rises a new phoenix, making it a symbol of immortality.

The Unicorn

There are many superstitions about this beautiful creature of myth. Only a pure young girl could catch it, with a rope of grass. It could purify poisoned water by dipping its horn in it. One odd story says its greatest enemy was the elephant. If a unicorn saw an elephant its usual gentle behaviour changed, and it fell into a violent rage.

FRANCE

▷ THE RO-BEAST ◁

Each night one of the villagers had to keep watch and wake the others in case of danger. Everyone feared fire, flood and storm, but there was one thing worse than any of these. The watchman knew what to listen for.

One night, the salty wind rose up and the waves roared as usual. But they could not hide a more sinister sound. The watchman recognised it at once – a heavy, rattling breath. The Ro-Beast was out hunting.

The men had seen the creature only once, but could never forget the sight. It was a huge, winged dragon with a scaly tail, and it came from the fiery depths of the earth. It was a cunning creature that trapped its prey with devilish tricks. It might pretend to be asleep, or dead, or howl as if gravely wounded. Some-

times it lay in the sunlight so that its scales looked from a distance like precious jewels. Then, when people came near, it would strike.

The watchman went to wake the others. They gathered up their weapons – stone axes, heavy clubs, and a few clumsy bronze swords – and sat around the fire to wait. They dared not attack the Beast, but at least they could defend themselves and their families.

They looked out over the sea towards the Beast's cave. Among the sounds of the storm, and the Beast's angry snufflings, they heard human voices. Surely this could not be? Was it

Seven strange sailors trapped the beast and turned to stone.

another of the Beast's tricks? A small, well-armed party went down to the shore to find out.

Down on the beach there was a strange boat. It was bigger than any they could build themselves, and obviously made for long sea voyages. Where had it come from, and where were the crew?

They were a little farther down the coast, near a deep hole in the rocks, facing the Beast. There were seven of them, and they were armed with bows and arrows. Each had a different target. Two aimed at the Beast's eyes;

two at its nostrils and two at its ears. The seventh aimed at its mouth. They all shot together, and none missed.

The Beast howled in pain. Unable to see, hear or smell anything, it rolled over and fell into the hole. The strangers stood in a circle, still as statues, on guard around the hole.

The men hurried back to the village, with the news that the Beast was trapped. It is still there today, and you can still hear its agonised roar. Around the hole where it is trapped, there stand seven tall stones.

▷ LUG'S BIRDS ◁

One winter morning, the king of Ulster and his guests, the most powerful lords of Ireland, were wakened by strange music that seemed to come from the sky. They went out and saw flocks of big white birds flying overhead, singing melodiously. The birds flew in pairs, each two linked by a golden chain. In the cloudy sky, there were nine flocks of twenty birds each. Where had they come from?

As the king and the lords watched, all the birds landed and began to eat the grass. In less than an hour, they had eaten so much that the king's rich pastures were reduced to a stony wilderness. The beautiful creatures were as bad as locusts. They must be hunted down, or all the people would starve. The king ordered his men to make ready nine hunting-chariots.

Each of the lords was to pursue one flock and bring the birds down with spears or with catapults. The king and his sister led the hunt. The party hunted all day, but never saw one of the mysterious flocks. Night came, and snow began to fall. The hunters were too far from the castle to return through the snow. They found a little cottage, and begged the couple who lived there for a night's hospitality.

They hunted all day but never caught sight of the magic birds.

The cottage was small, most unfit for a king and his retinue. But as they entered, it seemed to get bigger. There was plenty of room for all, and stables for the horses. In the main hall, they found a rich feast waiting. They realised that this was a magic hall of the gods.

That night, the king's sister had a strange dream. Lug, god of light and life, appeared and told her the secret of the strange birds. 'They were my messengers. I sent them to draw you to this hall. Soon you will know why.'

Next morning, the party returned home. When they looked back at the site of the magic hall it had gone. But the king's sister was pregnant; nine months later she gave birth to Cuchulainn, one of the great heroes of Ireland, and the son of Lug.

▷ ROUGHPELT ◁

A wandering knight sat in an inn in a small French town, enjoying a warm fire and a mug of cider before going on his way. It was market day, and both the inn and the narrow streets were full of people: buying and selling, gossiping, or just having a drink and a bite to eat.

Suddenly there was uproar in the street outside: screams of fear and panic. A crowd rushed into the inn. 'Roughpelt!' they cried. 'He's here again!' The landlord locked the doors and windows, and everyone huddled together in a corner of the room. Outside, the streets were emptying, as everyone hurried to find safe shelter anywhere they could.

The knight stood by a window, and thought he heard something outside: harsh breathing, and a heavy tread. He told himself not to be a fool. 'Panic is infectious.' But then he saw something like a huge bear, carrying off a cow. It stopped briefly by the inn door, then headed slowly away.

The knight asked the innkeeper what the monster was. 'He's a creature of the devil,' said the man. 'A monster that devours people and animals. He lives in a waterfall, and his hair is always wet and tangled, so we call him Roughpelt. Nothing we do will make him go away.'

The knight had an idea. On the way to the town he had passed the pope's envoy. 'A holy man like that must be able to drive an evil spirit away.' So, when the envoy arrived, the towns-people were waiting for him. He seemed reluctant to try, but at last agreed to go with them to the waterfall, where he said a prayer. Roughpelt rose up out of the water and growled, and the envoy fled. Back in the town he admitted that he could do nothing: he was in a state of sin. Only that morning he had kissed a young girl.

Undeterred, the people asked the parish priest, the deacon, and even the bishop. But none of them succeeded: one ate too much, another drank, another was lazy. In the end all the clergy in the district had tried, but for one, Father Martin. He was a quiet, simple man who spoke to the monster gently. Roughpelt left the waterfall and followed him into the town.

At last they reached the church. Father Martin made a sign; and the monster turned into a statue. The people were free, and the statue stands to this day.

*Only pious Father Martin could persuade
Roughpelt to follow him.*

*The Sphinx
of Thebes.*

▷ THE GUARDIANS ◁

There are many legends in which fabulous beasts are guardians of treasure. Sometimes these are piles of gold or jewels, sometimes fountains of youth or trees of knowledge. The guardian beast is often only the last of many perils the hero must overcome to win the treasure.

But even everyday creatures can play their part in legends. Irish tales tell how cats guard ruined castles, watching them silently all night, because they can see in the dark.

At the gates of the city of Thebes lived the Sphinx, a winged monster that was half woman, half lion. The Sphinx challenged all visitors to the city, asking them a riddle. If they got the answer wrong, she ate them. The riddle was: What has one voice and yet becomes four-footed, two-footed and three-footed? Only Oedipus got the answer right. It was man who crawls on all fours, then walks on two legs and

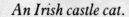

An Irish castle cat.

1 Two griffins, birds with the bodies of lions and the wings of eagles, guard the god Apollo's treasure in Greek legend.

2 The Celestial Wolf of Chinese legend guards a god's palace in the constellation of the Great Bear. It is represented in the sky by the bright star Sirius. It catches humans who come too near and flings them down into a deep gulf.

3 The Hydra had three heads, one of which was immortal, but Heracles managed to cut off all three.

4 Eating the flowers of an ancient Persian tree of life brings eternal life. But, just in case humans should try to gather them, a horrible giant lizard guards the tree – and swallows all the flowers as they fall.

5 Western dragons often sleep through the centuries guarding piles of gold. But it would be a foolish hero who assumed a guardian dragon would sleep through an attempt to steal treasure! Better to lure the creature from its cave, and try to stab it in the weak spot every dragon has somewhere on its body.

6 The naga serpents of India carry their treasure, precious stones, on their heads. Only the bravest of heroes would dare risk their poisonous bite.

then needs a walking stick in old age. The Sphinx was so furious that she hurled herself from the high ground where she lived to her death.

ANIMALS OF FACT AND FICTION

All over the world there are stories about animals, from Aesop's Fables to twentieth-century creations such as Richard Adams's *Watership Down* or Walt Disney's *Bambi*. Many of these stories feature animals that exist in the real world. Others tell of fabulous beasts, creatures of the imagination.

Creatures of chaos

Many fabulous beasts are terrifying. They represent forces in the world that humans cannot control. The dragons of Western legends, with their fiery breath, armoured skin and voracious appetites, are the prime example. Dragons are often shown as living in caves deep under mountains, sometimes guarding treasure. They feature in Christian legends as representatives of the devil, or the forces of evil. The destructive dragon killed by St George is one example, and the many-headed Beast in the Book of Revelation is another.

Cold-blooded monsters

With their scaly skins, dragons look more like reptiles than any other living animals. But why should reptiles represent evil? Though there are some poisonous snakes in Europe, most reptiles are tiny, shy, inoffensive lizards. With their cold blood, they are not warm and pleasant to touch like mammals; they are not good to eat; and they creep along the ground silently, or hide themselves away. Perhaps people thought that they came from hell.

Once many people believed that hell and dark 'subterranean' forces were under the ground and might break out at any time and destroy them. Mysterious caves, fissures in rocks where steam rose up, deep potholes and even hot springs all seemed like entrances to this terrifying underworld – or exits from it. Tales of brave heroes who killed creatures from this world were reassuring, as well as exciting in themselves.

St Michael takes on the beasts of hell.

such stories kept the danger in the crews' minds, and perhaps made them sail more carefully.

Lurking in lakes and rivers

Rivers and lakes also often have legends about fabulous beasts. Large rivers, such as the Amazon, which are the local people's main source of food and means of transport, are often said to have guardian spirits. Waterfalls and rapids – dangerous to small boats – are sometimes haunts of monsters, whether in Africa (the Chipique of Victoria Falls) or France (Roughpelt). One of the most famous lake monsters is a modern one – the Loch Ness Monster of Scotland, hunted since the 1930s by eager photographers and film-makers, but still elusive.

The story of Jonah and the whale, as portrayed in a medieval manuscript.

A giant octopus rises up to crush a seventeenth-century sailing ship.

From the depths

The sea, too, is full of mystery and danger, and was even more so in the days before big ships and accurate maps and charts. Sailors, at the mercy of wind and tide, sometimes drifted far from their course, and some never returned home. When people who usually sailed close to the coast found themselves far out to sea, they might see huge whales or even flying fish; things that would amaze their friends at home. Real sea creatures sometimes appear in legend either at exaggerated size (such as the giant octopus), or doing impossible things. An example is the Bible story of Jonah and the whale; no whale could possibly swallow a man whole. Fishing-boats sometimes caught creatures their crew had never seen before. So it was easy to believe in such dangerous marvels as the Kraken or the sea-serpent.

Even close to land, the sea is dangerous. Rocky places, whirlpools and hidden shallows have taken many sailors' lives. Often legends grew up about a particular, dangerous place along the coast. Besides offering an explanation for (perhaps) a strange-shaped rock,

Half and half

Among the water-creatures is the mermaid, also one of many legendary part-human creatures. There are stories of mermen, too, but it is the mermaid who has caught the imagination of the world. Her place in legend may start with the Greek Sirens, bird-women who sat on a lonely Mediterranean rock singing seductively to lure sailors to their deaths.

The more recent mermaid has a fish-tail, and stuffed 'mermaids' were sometimes displayed in fairgrounds. They were, of course, fakes: the top half was a stuffed monkey, the bottom half a stuffed fish. In sailors' folklore, to see a mermaid (often 'with her comb and her glass in her hand') meant storm and shipwreck lay ahead. But in spite of that, modern people tend to see the mermaid as a friendly character, quite unlike the sinister Sirens.

Other part-human creatures include the Greek and the Egyptian Sphinxes, both mysterious creatures with a lion's body and human head. The Great Sphinx near the Egyptian Pyramids at Giza has the face of Pharaoh Rameses II, and is an emblem of his royal power. The Greeks also told tales about the Centaurs, men with the bodies and legs

The gentle unicorn is a favourite royal emblem. Here the beast is depicted among fruits and flowers and wears a jewelled necklet.

of horses. They were renowned for their wisdom and learning – but also for drunkenness, lustfulness and starting fights!

Creatures of charm

Not all fabulous beasts, as we have seen in this book, are frightening or sinister. The unicorn is perhaps the gentlest beast in Western mythology. Its horn was said to have magic powers, and (like the stuffed 'mermaids') fake unicorn horns were sometimes a source of money for sailors. The long, twisted horn of the narwhal would deceive most land people!

The cruel dragons of Western mythology would not be recognised in China or Japan, where dragons are usually friendly spirits that benefit humans. Despite this, Eastern and Western pictures of dragons often look very similar. The artists of these cultures were inspired by similar reptiles, but the stories they illustrated were very different.

Are there any beasts out there?

As the world has become less mysterious, the human delight in imagining strange creatures has not gone away. But in some cases, the terrifying creatures have simply been placed on other planets. 'Creature features', films such as *The Creature From The Black Lagoon*, were a craze in the 1950s. Often the monsters in them were said to be a result of genetic mutation after a nuclear test, revealing people's anxiety about new weapons and the domination of science in modern life. Strangely enough, all the 'creatures' in these

A friendly dragon keeps watch at the entrance of the imperial palace in Beijing.

films, however bizarre their stories, either had one head, two arms and two legs, just like humans, or were gigantic insects. Special effects were in their infancy, so it was a choice between projecting a film behind the actors, or dressing an actor in a rubber suit. (It was cruelly said that you could sometimes see the zip!)

Outside Hollywood fantasy, however, some people claim to have seen 'monsters' – or at least, large unknown

creatures – today. Besides the Loch Ness Monster, there are the Yeti of Nepal and the Bigfoot of North America, both described as resembling either large upright apes or large, very hairy, humans. Both live – if they live at all – in wild, inaccessible areas.

Occasionally, people claim to have seen animals thought to have been extinct for a relatively short time. One possible survivor is the thylacine (or Tasmanian Wolf), a strange, dog-like marsupial found on the island of Tasmania. It probably survived into the twentieth century, so perhaps it is still with us. There are also reports of moas, giant flightless birds from New Zealand, but the most recent one was proved to be a hoax.

However, new animal species are discovered every year – though most of them are insects. If an animal is big enough to eat (or to make someone afraid of being eaten) the people living nearby usually know about it. Still, you never can tell. . . .

A medieval picture of Pegasus, the winged horse from Greek myth.

A Roman mosaic depicts an underwater Centaur and a dolphin.

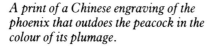

A print of a Chinese engraving of the phoenix that outdoes the peacock in the colour of its plumage.

47

▷ INDEX ◁